The Embodied Groomer

Cultivating Power and Presence
back into your work

ANNIE ROSE WRATHALL

"Dedicated to the healing journey, both within ourselves and with the animals we love."

"For Charlie, and all those whose unwavering support made this journey possible."

"To my boys Remy and Saylor, who were my first teachers on working with dogs, and the love and dedication needed to evolve into being a better self."

The journey of a groomer extends far beyond the clippers and the shampoo. It's a delicate dance of skill, empathy, and resilience, often performed under the watchful eyes of both pets and their owners. But what happens when the stress of the salon begins to take its toll? When the daily triggers and emotional burdens start to weigh you down?

That's where this book, "The Embodied Groomer," steps in. It's more than just a guide; it's a lifeline. Annie has crafted a powerful resource born from personal experience, a testament to the transformative power of self-awareness and healing.

In these pages, you won't find quick fixes or superficial advice. Instead, you'll discover a profound exploration of how to navigate the emotional landscape of your profession. You'll learn to recognize your triggers, to understand the bodies response to stress, and to cultivate a sense of inner peace amidst the chaos of the salon.

Annie's commitment to sharing practical tools, including Somatic and CBT techniques, underscores the importance of holistic well-being. This book is an invitation to embark on a journey of self-discovery, to redefine your relationship with your work, and to create a more fulfilling and profitable career.

Whether you're a seasoned groomer or just starting out, "The Embodied Groomer" offers valuable insights that will resonate deeply. It's a reminder that true success begins from within, and that by prioritizing our own well-being, we can create a ripple effect of positive change in our lives and the lives of those we serve.

Prepare to be inspired, to be challenged, and to emerge with a renewed sense of purpose. This book is a gift—a testament to the power of self-care and the transformative potential of an embodied life.

Table of Contents

CHAPTER 1 In The Beginning 9

CHAPTER 2 Plan For Success 23

CHAPTER 3 How Are You Showing Up 37

CHAPTER 4 Change Your Paradigm 63

CHAPTER 5 Selfcare 73

CHAPTER 6 Rebuilding Trust 85

CHAPTER 7 Not All Dogs Are The Same 99

CHAPTER 8 How To Set You Value 107

CHAPTER 9 You Did It 117

CHAPTER 1
In The Beginning

When the man walked up he said,

"What is Wild Dog doing here?"

And the woman said,

*"His name is not Wild Dog anymore,
but First Friend, because he will be our friend
for always and always and always"*

-Rudyard Kipling

The purpose of this book is to help you become an embodied version of yourself. I will give you tools to gain self awareness and an inward view of the blindspots that exist within you. There are sections of deep reflection which will require compassion from yourself to be honest and an opportunity to change. After many years of inward work, I have found a path that has proven to be helpful in my work with animals. It has given me a chance to deconstruct my old ways, and create a new way of being.

This has increased client loyalty, brought in higher profit, and made my career fulfilling. I believe it is important to share the wisdom we gain with others. So we may all rise together. Working with animals has been a lifelong path, and for many of us, it came from childhood dreams. Together we can change the grooming industry and make grooming something people trust in. We can rebuild the trust of our clients, and create something special between us and our clients. And it all starts within.

Below is a typical day in many shops. Have a read, and feel what comes up within. We will use this story later to tap into self awareness. When you read it, take note of how your body feels. This is a response affecting your whole being daily.

Let me begin by painting a vivid picture, a story familiar to countless groomers. Imagine a typical midday scene in a bustling grooming shop: the incessant buzz of the phone, a chorus of impatient client calls about late pick-ups, a swirling blizzard of fur clinging to every surface, the staccato bark of anxious dogs, the relentless whir of industrial fans trying to combat the oppressive humidity, and your own eyes, heavy and strained, your body a symphony of aches and pains.

You drag yourself to the kennel, where Cleo, a 22-pound terrier mix, has been languishing for the past hour, supposedly drying. But instead of a fluffy, ready-to-go pup, you find a trembling, incessantly barking creature, his fur matted with excrement he's tracked through. The stench hits you like a physical blow. A sharp, searing pain radiates from your lower back, a familiar reminder of the physical toll this job takes. Your shoulders tense, mirroring the tension in Cleo's rigid body. Another bath. Another delay.

You crank up the music, a desperate attempt to create a buffer against the chaos. Lady Gaga's throaty vocals blare, 'Rah rah ahh ahh ahhhhhh,' a sonic assault that mirrors the sensory overload in the room. Without thought, you put Cleo in the tub, pour on shampoo and spray him down for the second time. You are completely unaware of his terror, his squirming or how you're handling him. Or maybe it's fair to say, you don't care, because you're not physically hurting him. Why is he even panicking? You're a nice person, everyone loves you with their pets.

So you wrap a towel around Cleo, grab him and put him on a table. You turn those tunes up louder, so you can focus on the music while you blow dry Cleo with the high force dryer turned on. Here is 22 lb Cleo, neck tied up in a grooming loop, air hitting his body all over, while you work away, with energy that is disconnected and inattentive to his needs. It's so loud, the smells overwhelm his system, and he begins moving his body, trying to find his internal calm place, to be that "good boy" his owner knows he is. He can't seem to shake or move himself around enough to release all the adrenaline that's been dumped into his system. Things shift. He feels your energy getting frustrated, as you are being forced to watch him more, because he is not standing still. Instead of standing still, Cleo is now trying to get out, bringing his front legs up to use his dew claws to pull the loop off. He wants to get away. He wants to avoid this current moment. Biting at the air, at you, at the chaos all around. And so, you turn off the dryer, grab a muzzle, throw it on him, firmly command him to stop it, and go back to drying him as you sing along to Gaga.

You won. He can't bite, he can't get away, what can he do? He watches, and holds this moment in his body as a traumatic event. The adrenaline pumping through him is marking this physical moment, and he instinctively can't help but move- but is so restricted. The battle begins between his mind and body. You're unaware of the internal process, you're unaware of all of this, because you are on autopilot. Why can't the dog just be good? You're a good person.

You catch the time. You're only 22 minutes behind. That time can be made up. Throw the stand dryer on him, and grab another high velocity dryer. Bam. He is dry in what seems like seconds, except for his insane amount of drool. You blast his face with the dryer, and make a mental note to groom Cleo's face first, so that you're not working with a wet muzzle before he drools on it again.

His owner is supposed to be coming at 2:30 and already it is 2:10pm. Time is feeling tight. Muzzle off, he is not trying to bite for the moment, but Holy shit he lays into barking. Because of his attitude, you decide to just clipper his face. No way are you putting your hands or scissors near this crazy dog that was trying to bite, and is obviously still aggressive and unmanageable. Your ears are ringing from his barking, so you grab a closed mouth muzzle and put that on him so you can finish his groom in peace.

Today is your lucky day as Cleo's owner is late, and you get him done at 2:35. Finally, the last dog of the day is done. You put his collar on him, and his leash, and you put him in a kennel until his owner arrives. A moment to finish your cold coffee from the morning, and ruminate on how bad of an owner they must be for having a dog that acts like this, and how they are late yet again- even when you specifically said pick up is for 2:30pm. Your body aches, and is stiff. You don't even know what you look like, because you haven't gone to the bathroom since 4 dogs ago- which was sometime around 9:30 am.

In walks Cleo's owner. A smile comes on your face. You wave at the owner, and say you will go get him. Into the back room to grab him from the kennel, pull off the muzzle quickly and stick his face under the stand dryer to dry and fluff up the flattened down hair... Cleo smells his owner, and goes into full on excitement mode. *His freedom is finally here!* You set him on the floor, and let him rush to the gate in the main room. He is jumping and barking with excitement. His owner is so happy to see his tail wagging. The smile that you painted on your face is large, but your dull tired eyes tell another story. You open the door, and Cleo runs around his owner. He flops on his back, and pees on himself. He is barking, and his energy looks to the owner as though he just loves her soooo much. You settle the bill with her, and tell her how good of a boy he was. The owner goes on her way, Cleo pulling her as fast as he can toward the car.

You stand for a moment, and drop your shoulders. You lose the smile, and think "*Thank fuck this day is over.*" It's 3pm now. You have been in this shop, doing this on repeat, since 8am. 5 days a week. As you look around, you see the other two groomers finishing up. Hair is all over the floor. You put your tools back in your tool box, and decide that you can clean in the morning. Gaga has switched to the news. Your mind is wandering to all that is going on that is beyond your control. You just want to go home, and forget about your day. "*Just two more days left in this fucking week, and then I'm off for two days*", you tell yourself.

Glimpsing in the mirror as you head to the bathroom, you see dog hair stuck in your messy ponytail. Your shirt is covered in hair, and a layer of fuzz is on your shoulders from the husky whom you did a blow out on first thing this morning. Mascara is smudged around your eyes, and the morning dream of today being a great day has failed. You now look as though you were dragged through Hell. You tell yourself to pee quickly and then get out of here. Maybe you can swing by a drive-thru for a burger, and get home early enough to get to watch a few episodes of your current binge show.

Thoughts begin.

'*Shit. When was the last time I peed today,*"

It's dark yellow.

Note to self, bring more drinks tomorrow.

"*Fuck, I hope tomorrows' dogs are easier.*"

Deep inhale, deep exhale.

Now what the hell was that day about? It's the kind of day that is on repeat for many groomers. Some days may be slower, some busier. But working steady, while mentally offline, is common. And it doesn't have to be.

Who am I to tell you that the pet grooming life can be easier ?

I have been a person similar to the one in the story I just described. While in training, I remember working non-stop, no dogs in kennels, but all running free on the floor. Stepping in poop, peeing, and barking, it was all the norm. Because they are animals, and interacting, and that's just how it is. It's not good or bad, IT JUST IS. But it doesn't have to be.

I have been professionally grooming since 2010. My life philosophy of work is smarter not harder. Through the years I have dug deep into understanding how to make grooming easier. How to earn more money and how to ease the load on my body. I've learned that a calm approach to grooming brings a much easier workday; happier client responses; and the dogs who learn to trust the process.

Shift your perspective, shift your life. An ethical grooming approach has helped me cultivate amazing client/owner relationships. My earning possibility has increased and overall work life balance brings joy to my life. My mind stays in a state of gratitude and abundance-even on the hard days.

This book is meant to help you gain the tools you need to shift your mindset, and regain your love of working with animals. It will help you look at your business practices, and show you how to show up with a new approach. It is written from a Therapeutic Somatic approach, helping you connect with mind, body and soul, which I have found to be the key to a fulfilling, happy life.

Who the fuck am I to tell you life can get easier? I have never lived your life, nor been in your shoes. But take a moment, and just read what I have to offer you. Maybe there is something to what I have to say.

I began my career in dog grooming with Tail Wagrrrs in Bedford, Nova Scotia. I was trained by instructors who felt that learning all aspects of working with dogs was important. Learning handling practices, behavioral language, and spending time in the doggy daycare helped create a well-rounded understanding of dogs' behaviors. The shop I was trained in did not believe in kenneling, so 4-8 students grooming, 2-4 staff teaching, and grooming in an active doggy daycare that often catered to 20+ dogs a day. It meant that it was busy, and many lessons were learned. Believe me when I say, I have learned a lot. Even when working with people who have kind hearts and good intentions, dog grooming can be exhausting and deplete the soul, if not managed with intention.

After graduating from the grooming program, I signed up with the International Professional Grooming Association. I began their training process to learn breed specific styles. During this time, I owned The Dirty Dog Shop, and I began shifting my view of what a grooming salon and environment could be like. I had gone against the old style environment. Everything was now visible to the clients. Glass doors, no kennels, and everything transparent. I wanted to have everyone who worked for me be accountable. When we are always being seen, we show up as our best selves, and find new ways to handle and work with dogs.

In my time of owning The Dirty Dog shop, I trained under Heather Logan (Creator of Pawsitive Directions Program at Nova Institute, and Cloverfield Animal Behavioral Services), and Silvia Jay (Trainer, and Author of Dump Dog), who came into my shop to help me find the best ways to work with dogs during the grooming process. I was informed that even though the dogs were being tolerant, and we were staying calm and doing the best we could, the dogs were still highly stressed. By having two separate trainers watch my processes, I was able to find a path which offered the dogs a more calming experience. Learning to read the signs helped me curate a way of being with the dogs and lowering their stress.

I was blessed to be in Truro, Nova Scotia, where some amazing dog trainers reside, and I spent time working with my own pets with Yan Mowat, of Little Moe's K9 Academy, and taking the classes offered there. I began noticing the more I learned dogs' language, the better the dogs I groomed responded, and the less stress occurred in the shop. Along with learning about them, I became reflective on myself, and saw how I could show up better. It was all intertwined, and I was on the path to healing inwardly and outwardly. I found the work I did to heal myself helped foster better relationships with dogs and their owners.

Since I first stepped foot in the grooming salon, I have learned so much that I never would have imagined. My professional background in Business and Marketing has helped me in creating a functioning business. Alongside, my personal experience growing up on farms around livestock and horses and seeing a range of training methods. The skills I obtained in working with dogs have come from never settling with what I was told, trusting in my intuition when things seemed misaligned and instead constantly seeking to improve. I strive to be my best, and if that means pushing myself in learning how to do a job effectively and efficiently, then I will find a way.

Through my career I have run three successful grooming businesses: A retail, grooming and consulting shop, a mobile grooming van, and I am now doing in-home grooming. I focus on dogs who require special attention who are anxious, aggressive or seniors. All the while, I always incorporate somatic practices, to maintain the energetic space I wish to create.

In 2024, I completed a Somatic Practitioner Program which I have begun alongside my grooming schedule, working with people in a trauma informed therapeutic approach. This is the job I plan to continue until I am on my deathbed. Grooming is taxing on the body, and therefore people often stop working this job in the later stages in life. I am a person who doesn't plan to retire. I love being busy, and enjoying every day, and not just working for future days. I love working with dogs and people. I love all aspects of life that provide learning.

Another identity I have is Mom. It is the greatest honour, guiding and bearing witness to my childs life while I am in this world. She has been in the shop with me since a week after her birth. She has grown up around dogs, and she shows me all the answers to being a better person, groomer, and to live with intent.

I don't know your own story, but I know where I came from, and I know it's possible to succeed. I know in the core of my being that if you change your mind, you change your reality, and you can achieve anything that you set your focus on.

This book is direct. I don't pussyfoot around on the steps it takes to succeed. If you are sick of dreading work and your life, then take responsibility for your learning and make a change.

Grooming shops can be unhappy places and they also can be a place of laughter and joy. You get to choose which shop you are running, by accepting it, you are complacent to it, and contribute to the problem. You can become part of the solution. That is where you become an alchemist. I can tell you-it's rarely the dog, but more the person who has handled them. 1 out of 100 dogs may be genetics, but the rest is how the groomer is working with the dog. Adjust your practices and you will see new results. This I guarantee!

This book will give you prompts to look at what is, and open your eyes. It will help you reflect on ways you can improve, and promote change within. Just for reading this far, I give you a fuck yeah high five!!! Let's do this!!

CHAPTER 2

Plan For Success

We can make do in life as we are. We can go about each day, having the affliction of life repeat itself, and the same emotions arise. Or we can make changes. If we change our perception, we change our reality, and our life.

What is your current perception of how you are and how you relate to clients and work?

Self reflection will be your biggest asset in life, and non-judgmental self reflection, even better. Having grace for who you were, who you are and who you are becoming is key. We do the best we can with what we know and have. And as the great Maya Angelou said "When we know better, we do better".

Your assignment is to paint a clear picture of how you are for your own review. To give you something to reflect upon. To understand what the reality is. So grab a journal and a pen, and write on the top of the page in bold letters

"HAVE GRACE FOR MYSELF".

And remember, that as you begin to answer these questions, you are evolving. Below I will ask you numerous questions, to help create an awareness of how you're living your life. Once we begin looking at ourselves , we can see blind spots and make changes.

Let's begin at this moment. Remove judgment, and see your reality for what it is.

Let's begin

I ask you to write out an honest snippet of you.

How do you see yourself?

How do you think others see you? (friends, clients, family)

How do you dress for work? What feelings arise when choosing clothes for the day? Is the outfit expressing who you are, and what you want to portray to the world?

Do you dress for the person you want to be, or the person of the now? Do you dress in a manner you assume groomers should dress?

Are you happy, content, and fulfilled? Or sad, dreading the day, and having low energy?

Do you treat customers with joy, or as a hassle? Are you energized to see them, or glum?

If you were a possible client and walked into your shop as it is at this moment- would you want to have your pet there? If so, write out what is working, and if not, write out what isn't working for you.

Are you nourishing your mind and body with healthy choices? Or are you consuming nutritionally void foods, and filling your mind with stagnant things like news, gossip, and distracting shows?

What are the daily thoughts in your mind?

Do you feel happy after completing a groom? Do you feel pride in your work?

Are you showing up the best you can?

Are there blind spots contributing to your lack of being where you want to be?

What kind of human interactions do you have in your life? In your home, work and social settings?

What are your current earnings? Are you satisfied with what you earn?

If you have employees or work with others, what is your standard way of being with them? What are the common conversations? What is the mood in the shop when everyone is together?

What type of clients do you attract?

How is the current state of your shop (state of equipment, smell of the shop, vibe of the shop? Is it organized, or in disarray?)

What is the current state of your car (is maintenance and upkeep done regularly, are engine lights on, what is the smell of the car, is it organized, or in disarray)?

What is the current state of your home (state of items you have, smell of the home, does it feel welcoming, organized, or in disarray)?

How is the current state of your life? Write out the first word that comes to mind.

Please take a breather and acknowledge the first step is complete. This is often the hardest for most people to do, as bearing witness to our own lives means we have to then be accountable. But when we become accountable, things begin to happen!

Life isn't about happiness, but now knowing your answers to these questions, are you okay with how you are at this moment? Is this the life of 8-year old you would have wished for? Is this the life of 80 year old you will look back on and be proud of?

Now grab a piece of paper and write this on it.

"There are only two people I need to make proud.

8 year old me and 80 year old me.".

Put this note anywhere you need the reminder. This phrase will become your inner guidance.

What this quote is asking of you, is to see the world with the clear eyes 8-year-olds have. They are curious about life, and loving, and playful. How would they respond to moments? Next look at the wisdom an 80-year old you would have. Appreciative of a life well lived, the ability to let go of all that is unneeded in life, and a general acceptance of what is. The only problem is how we live in between; with baggage, chaos and noise. Begin to think in these two mindsets, and you will see more clearly the wisdom of the child and the elder.

The above self reflection exercise is done twice, once at the beginning (right now) and again when you have finished the book, so that you can see how you have shifted your paradigm. At the back of this book you will have the same practice checklist. Try to be mindful each day to make the decision to be positive. So you can see that you're actually in control of your reality, and you can advocate for the way you control it.

Now let's dig deeper. Grab your journal again and write out responses to the following questions.

Where do you want to see yourself in 6 months, 12 months and 5 years from now (if there was a magic wand, where and who would you be)?

What skills do you have now?

What skills would you like to obtain in the future, in 6 months, 12 months and 5 years?

What are your weaknesses?

Are there things you feel you need to improve on? Are there things that can be taken over by another member of the team, or hired out for someone else to do? If not, then can you increase your skills, so they become strengths? You get the chance to change your reality by evolving skills and mindset.

Which clients bring you the most joy? I love to journal out my dream clients, and then I look at how I treat them, and I begin treating the others the same way. Very quickly the clients who weren't my dream ones, shift and become amazing. If we treat each client as our favourite, and only speak goodness of them, then they become that. Keep that in mind. Our thoughts become our reality.

What dogs are you best at grooming, and why? How can you get more of those clients, so you can be doing more of what you are best at?

What would you like to earn per day/week/month? How can you get to that rate? Adjust prices, upgrade skills, re-brand?

Are you working a schedule that feels good for you? If not, I ask you to challenge yourself and make a change. What are your dream hours?

Who do you think people see you as? How others see us does matter when running a business. Our unconscious mind is running maladaptive behaviors which we call personality and give blame to that, but the reality is, we are more than that, so when we unload the layers and show up as our whole selves, people begin to appreciate us for who we truly are. So who do you think they see?

Where are you now in life? Are you set up in a manner you're proud of, or is there more you would like?

Eyes Open, let's unpack more and make another list.

What am I wanting to not have in my life; how can I change that?

Write it in a manner of releasing.

I release all that does not serve me for my highest good.

I release my clients who bring unkind words to the shop

I release the dogs who don't align with me

I release anger that I hold inside

I release the feeling of self sabotage

I release the fear of not paying my bills

I release the overwhelming request of the clients

I release frustration I feel when friends ask me for discounts and I can't say no

Continue writing this list out until you feel like you have released all that feels binding.

Now I invite you to write a list of gratitude for what you have. Putting to paper what we have gives us the chance to see with our eyes the blessings before us. Some may have larger lists than others, but having gratitude for what WE have is key. You can desire more, but need to be grateful for what you have, or else nothing will satisfy. In this gratitude list, also write out what you wish to achieve, but write it in the present tense.

I am thankful for the high salary of $xxx,xxx that I earn.

I am thankful for my clients' appreciation of what an amazing service I offer.

I am thankful for the ease each day brings, and how it flows with joy.

I am thankful for my strong body that helps me do my tasks.

I am thankful for the overwhelming support of my clients.

I am thankful etc…

Now take a pause, and a deep breath. **Box Breathing** In for the count of four, hold for count of four, and exhale to the count of four, hold for the count of four and repeat.

Congratulations on the hardest part of this book. Even if it doesn't feel true now, write at the end of your notes- *I love myself for showing up and choosing to do this work.* These little reminders of self-love are very important. Training yourself to say it, will start the process of actually feeling it and embodying it.

Now realistically look at what you have written. How far are you from achieving your goals?

Do you see how you may be not fully showing up as your best self? Have grace for yourself.

Let's dig into making those goals a reality:

Step One: Take your list of goals. Number each one from most important to least important. Now take number one and write out the steps to achieve it.

Example

1. Earn more money per groom-

    What attributes do I need to be able to charge more, and have more money in my pocket after each groom? There is a psychological part in this that the client perceives value in a service only when certain factors are met.

Do you want to draw in a higher paying clientele? Then you need to look around your shop. Is it something you would see as a high value business? Is it clean, organized, un-cluttered? Does it smell fresh, and look visually appealing?If not, then make your sub-list.

What simple steps can be taken to increase the business aesthetics. *A paint job can do wonders for making a place look new. Closed shelving for tools, books, towels. Neat and tidy are more important than an expensive location.*

This can make the shop look more appealing. People pay more for what they view as high value.

2. I am going to upgrade my skills

   Are your skills where you want them to be? Charging more means offering better quality. You need to be offering something better than your competitors.

   Sub list:what overall skills will make me stand apart from the competition?

   Learn dog language, learn training basics, upgrade grooming techniques for smoother grooms, learn patience, emotional regulation, and mindfulness.

3. Expand my ability to better customer service.

   Is your customer service excelling? Are you getting referrals? Do clients rebook, so they hold a spot with you, or is it a last minute thought?

4. Become comfortable being my authentic self with clients.

   Are you an authentic person? YES this matters. People sense when someone is not being authentic, and when they do, they feel distrust, and they will leave. So be honest, and authentically you. Be honest with clients. I hear it all the time: Susie says Fluffy is good most times, but when I meet Fluffy, instantly I can get a read on her that she is anxious, and terrified on the table. And the owner doesn't know because the former groomers were never honest about that. When I tell them the truth that Fluffy is a, b, c, they breathe a sigh of relief that they weren't going crazy and that they can trust their intuition. They respect me for being honest. The clients will learn to respect your words as well.

Continue on with your list of goals until you have written out the steps needed to achieve them.

Excellent Job!!

Now that you have written out who you are in this moment, you have gained awareness and insight to where you want to go. You have brought attention to your strengths, weaknesses. When we know who we are, we can address our issues and become who we want to be.

These steps are here so that you can honestly look at yourself. Often we settle with what is, and we don't reflect on what we want to change or who we could be. You have now written out the full scope of what is happening in your life.

Take a moment, close your eyes and thank yourself for your honesty for looking at how you are showing up in this current moment. It takes courage to look within.

CHAPTER 3

How Are You Showing Up

How we show up in our day, begins in the first moments when our eyes open. We set the tone with our mindset.

Start your day right and make the most of the present moment. Becoming the alchemist of your life, means turning what you have into magic, which will transfer to your clients and all those in your life. To do this, we need to look at ourselves with aware nonjudgmental eyes, which we have been doing in previous chapters. This section will take you through distress tolerance, judgment awareness, mindfulness, and emotional regulation.

You have the lists you wrote out in the previous chapter on the reality of how things are in your life.

Now to make a change, you need compassion for self, and grace during this time. We can intellectualize things, but to integrate them, it takes practice. The first step we did was awareness of what is. Next, we must make the decision to change, and integrate these changes into our daily lives.

Groomers have many different perceptions, often depending on who trained them, and the atmosphere they are in. It is a high stress job, if not handled correctly. We need to learn that one person being angry can transfer into everyone in the shop, and cause horrible energy to work in. It is more harmful to stay in anger, hurt, and dark emotions, then to be in light.

So to handle yourself one must look inward, and make a conscious choice to change their response. A trick for when emotions arise is to feel them. When we resist, they persist. When we feel emotions they dissipate.

Let's practice.

Recall a time when you were frustrated.Like the story in chapter 1. You had a dog squirming on your table, not complying to your needs, tilting its head every time you went to hold its chin to clip around the eyes. Trying to sit while you're shaving the feet.

You were in a time crunch, and you felt the frustration. Close your eyes, and feel that moment. Let it fill you. Expand that feeling throughout your body, and make it as big as you can. Imagine the frustration in your whole body, and be with it. Is there any noise that you want to make to verbally express this feeling? Guttural sounds, screams, moans, etc. release those sounds. *(when we allow sounds to come up and be released, we are releasing the held emotions we had repressed, it is essentially giving relief to the feeling, giving ease to the moment)*

Pause.

With closed eyes and still body, ask yourself, "*What do I need?*" Some may respond "I need the dog to just stand still", but that isn't the reality. The dog is responding from its reality of being an energetic being. So ask again, "*What do I need?*" Notice the first word that comes up, and get curious about it. Place a hand on your body where you feel it the most. Ask yourself again "*What do I need...?*" And when you get a response, breathe into your body to the count of four, hold to the count of four, exhale to the count of four, hold to the count of four, and repeat this three times. Feel the frustration dissipate, and thank yourself for looking inward.

Now when we go back to the squirming dog, we have our bodies' wisdom. We can see a new perspective. What did we need at that moment? Was it patience, a break, food, or did something else arise that wasn't even about that moment, but still came up and was calling you to take charge and change. If we begin to bring calm to our inner world, the dog senses that, and will respond accordingly. Sometimes it may take a few sessions for their nervous system to realign. By doing this exercise regularly, we will shift how the dogs respond.

Somatic therapeutic approaches work on an inward level to release years of repressed emotions. The emotions that we think no one sees, but everyone feels. If we are around other people with similar feelings like anxiety, they may not notice our off energy, but other people do and animals especially can feel your internal energy. It can be felt in your tone, your language, and how you hold your body. Doing Somatic practices overtime, your body will naturally begin to stand taller, and you will become more embodied. What I mean by embodied is that you will have a better sense of who you are and your own needs. You will know how to care for yourself in a manner that isn't self sabotaging. It is a daily practice, or a lifestyle may be a more correct way of thinking. This needs to be done in all avenues of your life. Your outside world is showing you symptoms from your inner world.

Preparing for your day is the first step in shifting your reality from what is to what could be.

How you plan your day is important, and it begins the night before. As you lay your head on your pillow, set your intentions for the following day. Let go of what happened today, as it is no longer in your control. Focus on the present and future. Think of how you will wake up, what you will wear, how you will feel. THIS MATTERS. This all matters because it is placing your energy from the outside world, back into yourself. Giving love to yourself and focusing on the most important person in your life- YOU. One must nourish their own soul, and give it what it needs. Naturally once your soul is nourished, the overflow will go onto others in your life.

The energy we put out comes back at us. Good or bad, it always returns. So set your perceptions to focus on gratitude for your life and career. This helps immensely.

If you are thinking "A*hhhh*, I have this bad dog, I have to deal with this rude client, or I hate my job," well then you are the cause of these problems;

for your perception is in the lack mindset, and therefore these problems will persist. You will continually welcome bad dogs, rude clients or shitty jobs. But you can change this by the way you think.

You can take control back, and shift your paradigm.

Let's break down what we have created within ourselves.

Distress Tolerance

When we are continually in environments that may be stressful, our body finds a way to disassociate to get through it. This builds a tolerance to what is happening within our environment and normalizes it. This often begins in childhood in our home environment. If one has been raised in a chaotic home, it feels natural to live life in such a way. The nervous system has been trained essentially to tolerate more than if you were in a calm environment as a child. Your body would respond to any distress and take action, vs a body that had normalized distress at a young age and the levels of tolerance became higher before they noticed the chaos. But that can be changed and you can begin to listen to your body and learn from it rather than ignoring it.

If you walk into work and see a bunch of stressed dogs and mess, does your energy drop, yet you are able to tolerate it? If so you have learned how to cope and tolerate distress by going into a down regulated response, also known as the fawn or freeze response. Alternatively if you walk into the same situation, and your body goes on high alert and you struggle to tolerate what is happening, this means that you are in an up-regulated response- also known as the fight or flight response. This means your nervous system is alert to the distress and is needing you to take action to bring your system back to a calm state. If your nervous system has a high distress tolerance then we need to build a new foundation and get the nervous system back online. We can't make changes if we can't see or feel it.

Our nervous system, if carrying undischarged stress, will show in two ways:

Sympathetic (Up-regulated) Symptoms

anxiety, panic, hyperactivity, exaggerated startle, inability to relax, restlessness, hypervigilance, digestive problems, emotional flooding, chronic pain, sleeplessness, hostility or rage.

Parasympathetic (down regulated) Symptoms

depression, lethargy, deadness, exhaustion, chronic fatigue, disorientation, disconnection, dissociation, complex symptoms, pain, low blood pressure, poor digestion

Previously we learned the technique of breathing and connecting to our inner self as a guide to bring us to a calm way of being. Now let's look at how to build up distress tolerance to what we see as acceptable. The breathing exercise will be a tool for you to use in moments when change is needed. Your body carries great wisdom, and when asked inwardly, it will respond. Trust in the answer that comes to you.

If you have been in a shop for years with no mirror on how you are, sometimes one will normalize how people are treating animals, and others within that space. You can't see the surrounding stresses, as it is the same every day. You become blind to reality. The good part is, your body and life will tell you if it is misaligned. Look at your energy, perspective on life, work and relationships. These core things, if there is heaviness or high energy when thinking about them tell us- we are in a distressed state and most likely have a high tolerance. One who lives in this state regularly will begin to show effects on the body such as adrenal fatigue. In this state it can and will bring illness to our body. The body's immune system will begin attacking itself because of the emotional state. The only way out is to make changes to our environment.(There are supplements that can be taken to help support the adrenal gland to offer ease while you begin this journey in healing.)

Begin to look at what needs shifting. The next phase is to expose yourself to the high and low feelings that arise while reviewing the items on the list you previously created. This allows you to learn how to shift feelings between the two internal responses. You can only shift if you have a visceral feeling to compare between what you have written to what you want the outcome to be.

Take the lists you previously made, sit on a pillow on the floor, or someplace comfortable, and look at what you have written. Flip it to the opposite, as if it is already done. If the shop is always messy, imagine it being clean. Close your eyes and feel in your body, what it would feel like to walk into a clean organized shop. How does your body feel with that? Do you feel more relaxed, calm, or overwhelmed by the steps to obtain it? Sit with your feelings for a few minutes, on the image of you standing in your shop, the clean floor, organized tools, a quiet space. Breath in deeply to that feeling, and when you exhale, imagine tension and heavy emotions leaving your body. Images or colours, can be attached to the thoughts. When exhaling them out, imagine them coming out in the breath. Keep this exercise up until it feels calm inside of you. This exercise is bringing you to an awareness level of what is a healthy nervous system response. Now take your mind back to the thought of your shop with hair on the floor, dirty tools, etc. And feel that in your body... Can you feel the difference? This exercise will show you the level of tolerance you have become blind to. Tolerating distress in your life will no longer feel the same as it once had, once you begin pairing the new technique to change what is to what could be. Your body will begin to seek the calm, and you will make changes to continue to have the calm. Extra effort will naturally happen for you to maintain that feeling, and your tolerance will lower, making more peace in your life.

Judgment Awareness

One needs to be able to look at themselves and see the judgment within before they can change it. We all have judgments on different levels. It is something taught to us at a very young age. When we place judgment on others, it is a sign of something that exists within ourselves that we have rejected. When we set judgments onto owners and dogs, we begin to dehumanize them, so that we can create separation of self. Instead, look at everyone trying their best. It may not be to your level, but it is their best they can do at that moment. *"We are all human, therefore nothing human can be alien to us." A quote by the great Maya Angelou.*

I will use aggression as an example of judgment, many groomers tend to misdiagnose dogs as aggressive, when in reality it is often miscommunication and fear being presented. Dogs rarely give their first reaction with aggression. A bite typically will be after many warning signs are given. We humans tend to not see the subtle language of dogs. That is why it is so important to be present and in your body awareness, so you can feel the shifts. I have never met a dog who wasn't warning me multiple times prior to an attempted bite. And even when they did make the bite action towards me, it was still a warning as dogs are spectacular marksman and rarely miss. The error we often make which increases risk, is to correct the bite with physical reprimand. This validates the bite, and will make them trust you less, and increase your risk of it happening again. A contact bite happens when all other signs have been ignored, and the dog feels it is the last resort.

Let's look over the information below to see how to handle our judgment on the experience of aggression.

Empathy First: Try to understand the root causes of a dogs symptoms before grooming. A dog groomer should see aggression as a symptom of underlying issues like fear or past trauma. By empathizing with the dog's feelings, groomers can approach them more effectively. When you approach situations with an open mind, and soft body posture, it can help the situation. Try using techniques to lessen the dogs stress, such as happy hoodies for the ears to quiet the dryer, and provide calming body language to the dog. Words aren't necessary, as dogs read body language before understanding our words. And one word used with different verbs can shift the meaning, so the dog may not understand. But if you use calming techniques, such as licking lips and looking away, this offers them support. A stressed dog will often yawn, lick lips, and shake to release the body response.

Professional Detachment: Listen to a client's dog's problems without judgment to provide unbiased support. Groomers should maintain emotional distance to remain calm and objective, ensuring they respond to aggression professionally. If a time comes when a dog does bite or show signs of aggression, don't take it personally, or as an attack on one;s character. A dog responds to miscommunication, not who you are; so adjust your practices by using tools to better support and create a safe environment and take nothing personal. Every dog can bite. Think of them as having a tolerance scale, and that all dogs start from different points. Some may live in a state of distrust and be quicker to react than others. Always watch the way you carry yourself, and the way the dogs body is set.

Positive Reinforcement:Ignoring unwanted behavior, you don't want is the first thing I teach. Any acknowledgment is a reward as it is attention given. Rewarding dogs for calmness or compliance during grooming encourages them to repeat those behaviors. If a dog tries to bite, turn away from them, and soften your posture, while holding firm. No physical reprimand is needed. Reprimanding with violence only makes them more at risk of biting. In a dogs mind, even if it bites first, and you correct them with violence, it validates the bite was warranted. An appropriate correction depends on the reason for the bite. If the dog is anxious, clearing your throat and continuing if safe to do so, is the best response. If aggressive, muzzle and continue, holding firm, yet calm energy. This is controversial and many may not agree, but it is my working philosophy that I have successfully used for my career. I have personally seen my clients turn from hard to handle, aggressive dogs, to lovely pets to groom. So that is enough for me to believe there is validity in this process.

Body Language Awareness: Use open body language to appear approachable to dogs. Groomers should also use body language that communicates calm and confidence to help reduce a dog's aggression. When greeting dogs in the shop, it is best to squat on the floor with your back to them, let them come to you when they are ready, and hold out a relaxed hand on the floor. Soften your gaze and don't smile or make eye contact. This subtle shift will change a lot of issues later during the groom, as the dog will have been given the chance to meet you in a manner that they understand. It is not submissive, but rather a neutral stance.

Patience and Consistency: Building a relationship requires patience and repeated efforts; similarly, establishing trust with a reactive dog involves consistent interaction over time. Not all people are the same, and that goes for dogs as well. Every dog we meet can learn what is expected of them, but they need a slow progression to build their nervous system up to tolerate the process.

Educate Pet Owners: Educate clients on the benefits of regular grooming and how it can reduce stress for their pets. Give yourself the agency to charge more for dogs that require more time. Most clients will understand and work with you for that. A dog that is groomed once a year does not build up the knowledge of what is going to happen each time. Often, they come to the shop in an uncomfortable state with new smells and noises. This can create fear and put the dog on guard. By working with clients to set regular schedules, you gain better clients. Those that don't want to participate, maybe can go elsewhere.

Seek to Understand: Gather background information before solving a case. Groomers should similarly learn about a dog's history and behavior triggers to tailor their approach for a stress-free grooming session.

Safety First: Like wearing helmets and knee pads for skateboarding, using muzzles or restraints during grooming protects both the dog and groomer from accidental harm if the dog lashes out. These are not to be used as punishment.

Professional Development: Learning to enhance your skills is important for groomers, updating their knowledge on dog behavior and grooming techniques to improve their service.

Nonjudgmental Communication: Offering constructive feedback without blaming helps groomers communicate with pet owners in a way that fosters understanding and cooperation. These explanations aim to provide a deeper understanding of each point, emphasizing the importance of empathy, professionalism, and knowledge in handling dogs during grooming.

What we judge in others exists within us. We can only see in others what we see in ourselves. It may be hidden in the shadows, but it is there. Write out a list of judgments and reflect within.

Judgments What I see in myself

How are these judgments affecting my life? What parts of my inner self did I close off because I was told they were not acceptable, and is that why there is judgment on another?

What would you tell yourself if you could speak with the child version of you? How would you help them step into a space of confidence?

Learning to rephrase the language to ourselves, can be a game changer

Mindfulness

Mindfulness in grooming is not just an afterthought. It must be the cornerstone of every interaction you have with both dogs and their owners. When you step into your grooming space, take a moment to breathe deeply and shift your mindset. This is more than a job-it's an opportunity to connect with another living being at a fundamental level. As you prepare your grooming tools, visualize each dog that will come through your door today. Imagine how your presence will affect their experience and how you can create a warm, welcoming environment that encourages trust.

Practice active listening with your canine clients. Pay attention to the subtle shifts in their demeanor—the way their ears perk, their tails wag, or curl tightly against their bodies. Each response is a key to understanding their unique personality and needs. For instance, a dog that flinches at a sound might need a gentler approach, while one that barks may just need a little reassurance. Likewise, fostering open communication channels with pet owners is crucial. When they describe their dog's quirks, validate their observations and offer insights based on your expertise. This not only builds rapport with the owners but also aids in tailoring a grooming experience that respects the dog's emotional state.

While you're cultivating mindfulness, consider the judgments that creep into your day-to-day interactions. Perhaps an anxious dog triggers memories of your own vulnerabilities. Reflecting on this can transform them from barriers into bridges of empathy. The child version of yourself would need reassurance, encouragement, and the freedom to express feelings—remind yourself to extend that same grace to your clients and the dogs. This practice will not only enhance your relationship with them but also nurture your own journey toward self-acceptance as a skilled and empathetic groomer.

How To step into the act of Mindfulness:

Lay your head on the pillow and close your eyes, tap into your imagination and fantasize about the perfect day.

You wake up, and feel light in your soul. The coffee smells especially delicious this morning. Your drive to work is smooth. The shop is clean and smells fresh. Your first client arrives on time, and the dog is receptive, kind and willing in the grooming process. Your clients' appreciate you, and come into your business with loving energy. Your pocket is overflowing with abundance. Your body feels great. Your mind is clear and you feel especially vibrant today.

Now repeat *"This is going to be a great day because I choose it to be."*

Your mind is what creates your reality, so take your power back.

Write out your dream work day: Create your reality by the power of intention. You get to choose how you respond to your day.

When I wake up in the morning, I awake with GRATITUDE. *(Copy this on a post it and put it on your bathroom mirror)*

"I thank the universe for the gifts I have received. I am grateful for waking up to this day. I see my efforts paying tenfold in return, I am grateful for the abundance in my life, and that I have the ability to see it unfold. I am grateful for the insight to see my clients as human, the same as I, and the dogs are innocent and behaving in accordance with their environment. I am grateful for the compassion that flows through my soul, as it helps me to be my best self"

Now set your energetic barrier.

What are energetics?

This is the energy we interact with as we move throughout the world. When we work closely with people, or animals, we are picking up their energy and wearing it. Although you cannot see it with your eyes, you feel it in your body. One person can shift our entire day if we are unaware. Over a day, we can be consumed with others' emotions, in such a manner we can't feel our own. So our body responds. This response can show up as anger, frustration, sadness, or irritability. Physical pain and illness can arise ((also1) And if we don't take accountability for this energy, it snowballs into a disaster and burnout.

So to set the day with energetics, close your eyes, imagine love flowing through you, and repeat this:

" *I place a golden dome around myself, within it resides love and light. I consent to peace . I do not take on anyone else's energy, it cannot penetrate my golden dome*"

As you say this, close your eyes and imagine your body being surrounded by a golden dome of love and light.

And to release anything that may have stuck to you throughout the day.

Sit in a calm quiet space, even in a

"*I consent to peace, I release all energies that are not mine, I breathe in love and light, and breathe out anger, fear, unhappiness. All that is within me nourishes my best self*"

Setting our mind is key to alchemizing what is to what can be, and in congruence to that we also need to set our physical spaces. Shop, home, etc.

When we leave the grooming space, we must prepare it for the day following, so cleaning our tools, the shop, it's all important. Promising yoursing you will always do your best, create patterns in your neurology and a new framework to work off of. Put up a list in the shop of what needs to be done before closing , and follow that list. On top of writing I *get to* "*do these items*. What thi"s does is shift reality, that you begin to think in gratitude vs lack. You get to be in a shop, own a shop or have a spot that pays you. You get to be trusted with peoples precious animals, and that says a lot about you. So see the gift life has given you.

If you work in a shop with others and their mind is not in the same place as yours, if you make changes in your space, and they see the shift in you, you will see they want that to change too. You will become the inspiration of change. People do better when they know better.

Sidenote: do you surround yourself with people who drain you, or those who enrich you? This is also an aspect of energetic boundaries.Humans often seek out others who can validate their behaviour, make sure you're around those that inspire you to show up as your best. Let's change the culture, day by day.

Emotional Regulation Techniques

When things get tough how are you equipped to respond? Great tools to bring our vagus nerve back to baseline is making the simple vuuu sound.

When we practice making the Vuuu sound, it taps into the vagus nerve , helping you remain calm when you're feeling stressed. The Poly vagal theory talks of this practice, by activating the sound Vuuu it activates the vagus nerve, restoring us into a regulated state.

Simply make a guttural sound of vuuu, as you exhale. Place a hand on your indent on the throat where clavicle bone indents. Adjust the tone until you feel the vuu sound vibration there. Three rounds of vuuus can bring you out of stress and into presence. Breathe in , exhale with the sound of vuuu, Breathe in , exhale with the sound of vuuu, Breathe in , exhale with the sound of vuuu.

These techniques are excellent for when our brain seems to go offline, and into a freeze response, and you need to regulate your nervous system.

Finger Grounding – put the fingertips on a flat surface, or somewhere on your body. Tap each fingertip, one after the other, and count 1,2,3,4,5, pause, 1,2,3,4,5. Counting can be silent or aloud.

Foot Grounding – press the feet into the floor. Tap each foot, one after the other, and say left, right, left, right (silently or aloud)

Stretch – Stand up, press your feet to the floor, and reach both arms to the ceiling, to the left, and then to the right. This can also be done while seated, if standing is not an option.

When anxiety, or are fawn, flight or fight response is triggered , we can add in one or all of the below exercises.

Self-hug – Wrap your arms firmly around your abdomen or ribs, curl forward slightly, and rock gently.

Head shaking – A few seconds of side-to-side shaking of the head, as fast as possible.

Scream into a pillow – Scream as loudly as possible, using a pillow or ball of cloth to muffle the sound.

Silent scream – Fill your lungs with air, lock the throat to prevent air entering the vocal cords, and scream fully

Exercise – Use large muscles in vigorous activity to burn through adrenaline – running, push-ups, kick-boxing, etc.

Submerge Your Face – Putting your face into cool water will trigger the mammalian dive reflex, which calms your nervous system to conserve oxygen.

Write it down/speak it aloud – Write in a journal or record yourself talking through the problem.

Sigh release – Breathe in as fully as possible, and sigh out with an audible "aaah" sound.

Blow release – Part your teeth slightly, purse your lips as though blowing out a candle, and blow air forcefully to empty the lungs. It can help to bend forward.

Kumbhaka breathing — Take a comfortable, full in-breath, hold for two seconds, gently breathe out all the way, hold for two seconds, and repeat.

Outward breathing — Breathe in swiftly, and make each out breath longer than the one before.

Deep breathing — Make each breath longer, slower, and deeper than the one before.

Practice and repeat

These tools will set your nervous system up to succeed in any situation. How you show up, will be improved once you practice and include the above practices into your daily life. When we know more, we can face anything.

CHAPTER 4

Change Your Paradigm

When you change your mind, you change your reality. Grooming can be fun, creative, and nourishing, even in tough times. It is up to you to change perspective and once you do then you are already taking action to shift your life.

Sometimes in grooming, we have one bad experience that colors all other situations to be the same. But when we dissect each situation, one can see each is different and it is an unprocessed experience creating these ideas.

Let's go through an exercise and see what arises. The practice is to see moments for what they are and transform your perception to what will serve you best.

Sample taken from chapter one.

The phone is buzzing, clients are late picking up their dogs, hair is all over the floor, dogs are barking, fans are running, your eyes are tired and your body aches. You go to pick up Cleo from the kennel he has been sitting in drying for the past hour, and he is shaking, barking steadily, and has shit and walked through it.

AHH you feel a twinge in your lower back, your shoulders tense, and now you have to re-bath this dog. You crank the music, having Lady Gaga belch out *Rah rah ahh ahh ahhhhhh*. Without thought, you have put Cleo in the tub spraying him down, and are completely unaware of his terror, the squirming and how you're handling him. Or maybe it's fair to say, you don't care, because you're not physically hurting him, so why is he even panicking? You're a nice person, everyone loves you with their pets. So you wrap a towel around Cleo, grab him and put him on a table. Turn those tunes up louder, so you can focus on that while you blow dry Cleo with high force turned on. Here is 22 lb Cleo, neck tied up in a grooming loop, pointy air hitting his body all over, a human with energy that is disconnected, and inattentive to his needs. It's so loud. The smells overwhelm his system, and he begins moving his body, trying to calm it, and be that "good boy" his owner knows he is. He can't seem to shake or move himself around enough to release all this adrenaline that's been dumped into his system. Things shift. He feels your energy get frustrated as you are being forced to watch him more, and he is not standing still. Instead, Cleo is now trying to get out, bringing his front legs up to use his dew claws to pull the loop off, he wants to get away, he wants to avoid this current moment. Biting at the air, at you, at the chaos all around. And so, you turn off the dryer, grab a muzzle, throw it on him, firmly command him to stop it, and go back to drying him as you sing along to Gaga..

You won. He can't bite. He can't get away, but what can he do? He watches and holds this moment in his body as a trauma response. The adrenaline pumping through him is marking this physical moment, and he instinctively can't help but move, but is so restricted. The battle begins between his mind and body. You are unaware of the internal process, you are unaware of all of this, because you are on autopilot. Why shouldn't the dogs just be good? You're a good person!

As you catch the time, you're only 22 minutes behind. That can be made up. Turn on the stand dryer and aim it towards him, and grab another high velocity dryer. Bam. He is dry in what seems like seconds now, except for his insane amount of drool. Blast his face with the dryer and make a mental note to groom Cleos face first, so then you're not working with a wet muzzle before he drools on it again.

His owner is supposed to be coming at 2:30, and already it is 2:10pm and time is feeling tight. Muzzle off, and he is not trying to bite for the moment, but Holy shit he lays into you barking, because of this you decide to just clipper his face. No way are you putting your hands or scissors near this crazy dog that was trying to bite and is obviously still aggressive and unmanageable. Your ears are ringing from his barking, so you grab a closed mouth muzzle and put that on him so you can finish his groom in peace.

Today is your lucky day as Cleo's owner is late and you get him done at 2:35. Ahh, finally the last dog of the day is done. You put his collar on him, and a leash, and put him in a kennel until his owner arrives. A moment to finish your cold coffee from the morning, and ruminate on how bad of an owner they must be for having a dog that acts like this, and how they are late yet again, even when you specifically said "pick up for 2:30pm." Your body aches, and is stiff, you don't even know what you look like because you haven't gone to the bathroom since 4 dogs ago which was sometime around 9:30 am, and in walks Cleo's owner.. A smile comes on your face, you wave at the owner, and say you will go get him.

Into the back room to grab him from the kennel, pull off the muzzle quickly and stick his face under the stand dryer to dry and fluff up the flattened down hair... Cleo smells his owner, and goes into full on excitement mode, *freedom is finally here* .. You set him on the floor and let him rush to the gate in the main room, he is jumping and barking with excitement. His owner is so happy to see his tail wagging, and the smile you painted on your face is large, but your dull tired eyes tell another story. Open the door, Cleo runs around his owner, flops on his back and pees all over himself. Energy that looks to the owner like he just loves her soooo much. You ring her up, tell her how good of a boy he was, and she goes on her way, him pulling her as fast as he can to the car.

You stand for a moment, and drop your shoulders, loose the smile, and think "*thank fuck this day is over.*" It's 3 pm now, and you have been in this shop doing this on repeat since 8am, 5 days a week. As you look around you see the other two groomers finishing up. Hair is all over the floor. You put your tools back in your tool box and decide you can clean them in the morning. Gaga has switched to the news, and your mind is wandering on all that is going on beyond your control. You just want to go home and forget about the day. "*Just two more days left in this fucking week and then off for two days*," you tell yourself . Looking in the mirror as you head to the bathroom, you see dog hair stuck on your messy ponytail, your shirt covered in cut hair, a layer of fuzz on your shoulders from the husky you did a blow out on first thing. Mascara smudged around your eyes. The morning ambition of today being a great day failed. As now you look like you were pulled through hell. You tell yourself to pee quickly and get out of here, maybe you can swing though for a burger, and get home early enough to get to watch a few episodes of your current binge show.

Above has set the mind for the below questions to be answered.

(Accepting moments and transforming distressing moments (CBT exercise) Journal the answers .)

*   Think of the above distressing situation, what happened in it?

    Ie.Outside circumstances- A lot of noise, fatigue, dogs distressed in kennels, and then rushed through the process. Groomer is hungry, so running out of energy. Distress tolerance is high, dog is stressed, overwhelmed and body has gone into an autonomic nervous system response by panting, drooling, barking, body movement, shop is messy,

* What past events happened leading up to this situation?

    Ie.The day was busy with other dogs. Loud shops all day, music that up-regulates humans and dogs to create a chaotic atmosphere. Unhealthy start to the day, preset mindset that you just need to keep pushing through and not stop to care for yourself.

* What role did you play in creating this situation?

    Ie.Not booking accurate time slots. Allowing the environment to be loud. Not regulating own emotions. Ignoring dogs' signs of stress. Not attending to the dogs stress signals

* What role did other people play in creating this situation?

    Ie.Clients late in picking up their dogs. You felt that your time wasn't respected. Not taking a moment to check in with Cleo to offer calm reassurance,

* What do you have control of in this situation?

    Ie.Emotional regulation, an ability to set boundaries with pick-ups, enforcing late fee if not there at specific time. Choosing to act in grace while working. Taking a breather between appointments so you show up grounded and dogs will feed off the calm energy, not the anxious.

* What don't you have control over in this situation?

    ie.Dogs response. Other groomers.

* What was your response to this situation?

    ie.Annoyed. Ignored everything around to just get through the day.

* How did your response affect your own thoughts and feelings?

    ie.Brought energy that made you feel down. Shut down so you could quickly work through the day.

* How did your response affect the thoughts and feelings of others involved?

* How could you have changed your response to this situation so it led to less suffering for yourself and others?

* How could the situation have occurred differently if you had decided to radically accept the situation?

It is very important to self-reflect and take steps to evolve your mindset. How you think may not always be benefiting you, so by looking at things with a neutral eye, one can see things from many perspectives and learn to live a life more aligned and at ease. Ultimately, if you're seeking success in all avenues- peace within is key. Financial abundance does nothing if you are suffering in the mind.

So do you want peace? If so, then make these changes to your lifestyle. Every aspect of your life is like a door into your brain, creating content that creates the way you view your reality. When one pauses though, and breaks down what is coming into our mind, we can see a lot of it is just noise. And we are often unconsciously moving through life with that noise. However, not you. You are seeing the reality of things now.

For a bit more reflection go back to Chapter two and the questions you answered in your journal. You have had some time to process what came up for you, what role you played, and what you wanted to change. Take notes and gain insight.

Hand on your heart, eyes closed and repeat "*I am proud of myself*"

CHAPTER 5

Selfcare

If you have gotten this far in the book, you are doing amazing!!!

Now let's see how you are keeping your mind and body nourished.

Look at the 5 point check in below and see what weak points come up.

Embodiment 5 Point Check In

Somatic Practice to begin to connect mind and body.

Focus and Clarity

Do you feel focused, clear, distracted, worried, angry? What is the state of your mind? Maybe it is curious? Without judgment, just be present with what is coming up.

Posture

How is my body sitting right now? Leaning forward, back, slouching, erect?

Sensation

Notice sensations - how is the state of your physical body? Notice what comes up with you. Sensations, areas of tension, temperature, areas of pain. Inviting more awareness to your own body, you might begin to notice what your body needs from you.

Breath:Holding or Restricting

No need to change breaths, but just become aware of it. Is there spaciousness and ease, or tightness and restriction? Take a deep breath and notice what arises as you bring more focus there. As we notice breath, emotional awareness can come alive.

Emotions

Feelings and associations- what is your emotional tone? Excitement, fear, disappointment, joy? Create more space and welcome all of them.

With this awareness, what does this part of me need and want me to know, and how do I hold myself in self-compassion and loving presence for what is?

Take a moment and write out how you feel now. *The feelings arising in this body are: tired, skin is dry and sore, back hurts, angry, desire for a change*

Now you have a current picture of where you are within your body. Once you have awareness, then you can begin to make adjustments, bringing you closer to where you want to be. These feelings that came up are showing you what needs to be changed. Love yourself for seeing this, and for the opportunity to make change.

Do you want to live a life like this? Is this your desired reality? If so, great, you're on the path to fulfilling your fate. If not, THEN LET'S MAKE A CHANGE.

I cannot express this enough, care for your well-being. If you have a sore back, rest it. Book smaller dogs, do whatever is needed to honor yourself. We are in the suffering mindset that groomers are tough and unbreakable. Grooming has a high burnout rate.

Signs you're burning out:

1. Physically and mentally tired. Your desire for life as it was, is dwindling. Social withdrawal.

2. Loss of passion. Losing passion for something you once loved to do is heartbreaking. If this happens, I suggest taking a step back and reassessing your processes to find love again. Loss of motivation to expand skills, monotonous days,

3. Feeling alone, annoyed at life, what you are doing, and how it has played out. Feeling like people think your job is all play and no one understands you or the demand

4. Crying easily-overwhelm can come out in tears,

5. Impostor syndrome- feeling like you have forgotten how to groom and the basics.

6. Feeling helpless-grasping to get through each day.

7. Feeling overwhelmed, resentment of the life you have. The demands of work seem no longer manageable, no longer have a desire to go to work and do your best.

If these resonate with you, here is what could be happening.

Causes for groomer burnout:

- Undercharging for services and overworking are a huge cause for burnout. Often groomers stack their day with too many clients, and get in the mode of fast turn around, with little to no time booked for breaks to regroup. Because the rate is too low (to keep customers happy) and the demand is high for groomers, we put ourselves last. The practice of stacking appointments to have one on the table, one in a kennel drying, and one on the floor, waiting. Often this means a perpetual cycle of rushing.

- Grooming dogs that require more time, whether it be large dogs, or dogs with temperamental issues can be a major cause for exhaustion. Focusing on one dog for two or more hours is tiring on the mind and body. This will cause an increase in fatigue, in which overtime adrenal fatigue can happen. Days when you have high risk dogs to groom (by this I mean anxious and/or aggressive) are mentally and physically draining. The body stays in a state of survival- whether it be fight, fright, fawn or freeze response, working with these types of dogs is harmful to your nervous system, and it catches up.

- Working alone- many groomers are alone, and during these times, have to do many tasks and wrestle with lifting, moving and caring for dogs with no assistance. In this case, they don't have anyone to talk to who understands, and so can feel alone.

- Poor boundaries with clients/coworkers- too much drama is brutal. It makes you sacrifice your needs for the needs of others. The days of people-pleasing need to end. Having coworker drama can turn one sour, and also make you resentful of clients, work and your environment. Set up your space for how you want to be, a peaceful space offers a peaceful mind.

    - For clients- have a rules list for what you will accept and not accept(it is up to you to set your boundaries), booking schedule, expectations of clients, rules for late or missed appointments, fees. You train people how to treat you. It is OK to have boundaries- actually it is amazing too. You set the stage! Don't tolerate rudeness. Act in a manner that offers grace, but have a no-bullshit attitude.

    - For Coworkers- don't engage in drama or gossip. When working with animals, we need a calm environment, and listening to Susie and her bf drama causes tension and brings unhealthy energy to a space. If Susie is having a hard moment- suggest a break to take deep breaths, shake it out, then pick up her socks and focus on the good while working. Our energy sets the dog's groom, If we are upset, guess what? So it is fluffy. She feels it, and although she can't explain why, she will be twice as antsy, nippy or whatever her stress response is. One bad apple spoils the bunch, so keep the garbage at the door, and people can pick it up when they leave at the end of the day.

- Working Conditions- if you have old uncared for gear, change it out. Your tools are what make your job easier. Good equipment means quality outcome.
    - High quality products matter. So does understanding the products you use, and how they can work for you.
    - Dull blades and scissors are unsafe. They make the job harder, and lower the quality and outcome of the groom.
    - Timing- booking a schedule that flows is important. Be realistic on what you can do in a set amount of time. If you know a dog

> is requiring more time, don't book a standard time in hopes that it will be different from every other time. Overbooking clients leads to stress, and actually slows down your work progress.

So many good groomers burn out because of these preventable things. Grooming is a mentally, and physically demanding job, so setting yourself up for success is important.

Now you can see what isn't working, and transform that into what is. Think of the opposing ways each shift can offer.

How to bring self care into your life.

Little steps become big strides. Caring for our mental state is important. Setting boundaries is a step in the right direction. Boundaries are not our words but our actions. You can tell others your boundaries, and then it is up to you to follow through with what you say you will do. So no large dogs, and someone books you a big dog. Simply say, I am not able to do this. I will have to cancel the appointment. Follow through with that. Each time we stand up for ourselves, we strengthen that muscle, and unconsciously build inner confidence and value.

We show others how to treat us, so if you allow people to walk over you, then they will. It is up to you to set how you want to be treated. Like the alpha dog- it is always the calmest, has clear boundaries, and doesn't need to be aggressive to get a point across. Only an insecure dog is aggressive and loud.

Another part of self care is making sure you're not overworking yourself. Knowing the hours you work best, and setting up a schedule to work for you is key. If you struggle with early mornings, then schedule afternoon appointments which allow you to be in a better state.

Self-care isn't just about taking a day for yourself, it is how you speak to yourself, how you overall care for your well-being. Remember a time when you felt the love someone offered you. What was it about their care that you appreciated? Offer that for yourself. Give yourself words of affirmation and supportive talk when you have done something. Even if you make a mistake, offer yourself love and kindness for your humanness. This is a way to heal and care inwardly.

Putting effort into caring for our mental health is important. Our mind needs love and attention as well.

Make a list for yourself- A love letter to yourself, all the things that you appreciate about who and how you are. Maybe you only have one or two things on it at first, but overtime keep adding to it. Watch the inner love expand, and witness yourself and your greatness. You are creating new ways to be in your whole self. Reconnecting with that part that we often shut out, so we can move through the world. But you don't need to, because when you come home to you a new world opens for you.

In the midst of your day, when the sound of clippers hums soothingly like a heartbeat and the fur swirls in soft eddies around your feet, remember to take a breath—not just any breath, but a deep, grounding inhale that feeds your spirit. As the sun filters through the shop's window, illuminating the motes of dust dancing in the air, acknowledge that this moment is yours. You are not merely tending to a dog; you are nurturing a connection, a partnership with each animal that enters your space. Your energy is a thread that weaves through their grooming experience, and by honing that thread—maintaining your focus, embodying serenity—you foster not only trust but also ease in the souls you care for.

You might recall how, during an unseasonably hectic day, a simple pause transformed everything.

Maybe it was that time you stepped outside for five minutes, and the cool air refreshed your frazzled mind, helping you return with renewed vigor. Embrace these moments of self-care as essential, not indulgent. Schedule them into your day as if they were appointments because in truth, they are. Each breath, each stretching of limbs serves as a reset, a recalibration that prepares you to face both canine and human clients with resilience, patience, and a calmer demeanor. Just as you would never send a pup back home unbrushed or unkempt, don't neglect your own maintenance.

Consider the lines of your love letter again. What would it say today? As you work through the grooming session, think of an affirmation to carry with you. "I am worthy of kindness, and I will cultivate that kindness from within." Over time, let these affirmations build a sturdy foundation for the respect you demand—not just from others, but from yourself. Each day is an opportunity to reinforce those boundaries. Grieve the tough clients, learn from them, but don't allow them to eclipse the joy in every wagging tail and gleaming coat. In creating a sanctuary for yourself, you transform your work environment, inviting not only the best version of yourself but also the best experiences for the dogs and their owners.

CHAPTER 6

Rebuilding Trust

This is your chance to step into alignment with clients.

The first step is to begin with honest communication to pet owners. Tell them your process in grooming, expectations, and then listen to their story. You need to speak with grace, to release judgment and try to understand the clients and their needs. By coming from a mindset of openness, it keeps their defensiveness down, and when they feel heard, you can move forward with an honest and integral relationship. Good clients appreciate and respect good communication. Some clients may not like it, which is good, because you are shifting those you allow in your life, and letting go of people who bring in drama. Someone who has boundaries knows to respect others, and those who have weak boundaries get bothered when someone does and will leave the situation. This is what you want , so you can draw in good clients who respect and trust you, creating a symbiotic relationship with the pet and owners.

Pets have become family. Their needs are listened to by the owners, and if the owner is dragging the dog into the shop, and it's shaking to be near you, you must self-assess what is causing this. Many of my clients have come to me with grooming trauma, they are nervous at first , but relax into my presence. They are happy to see me, but some never regain full comfort on the table. That is ok, as long as they are excited to be near me prior to the grooming process. This tells the owner that I am safe, and the dog trusts my being.

A dogs nervous system responds to similar situations it has been in . So you can retrain and heal part of it, but only once you have done that within yourself. We are the energy guides for these animals. We set the security within ourselves, and the animals will be drawn to it. Some may take longer to learn that you're safe, and that they will be ok through the grooming process.

Questions to look inward about are:

What does my energy feel like for me when this client is here? Is this for all clients, seniors, puppies, anxious or just the particular dog/client?

How am I showing up mentally and emotionally when I work with this client?

How is my shop when this dog arrives? Is it loud? How does it smell? Is it quiet, relaxing and fresh?

Now place yourself in the dog's spot. If you were taken to a place of discomfort, how would you like to be treated?

(Often people have this view that the dog should just be ok with the process if they aren't being physically hurt, but we forget, dogs are energetically sensitive and emotional beings. And the energy of the space matters.) I have been grooming dogs in clients homes for years, and the dogs love seeing me, but once some dogs get on the table, they still have a visceral response of shakes and barking . It is my job to make sure I am at peace within, so I don't get upset by their reactions. I explain the process to the owner, and hold no shame within for the dogs actions. Its nervous system is simply responding to experiences and it is through no fault of mine. This is only true if I am in alignment within myself that day.

An example is a Jack Russell Terrier named Penny that I work with. Her owner had taken her to a salon for grooming, but before he could get to his vehicle in the parking lot, he received a phone call that they needed him to come back and get her, she was too reactive. I got his message with warnings that she might be bad on the table, but I was willing to see what could be done to help her. I arrived, set up my table in the home and just ignored her. While Penny smelled around, I chatted with her owner. My conversations with new clients always go over my rules. I explain possible reactions a dog may have, barking, screaming, biting, squirming, pooping or trying to jump off the table. Then I go over my responses, that the owner isn't to come over to the dog while I am working, unless I request it, I explain that no matter what, do not correct the dog, I allow the dogs to go through their motions of stress responses. It is natural, and I want them to see that no matter what they do, I won't respond in aggression, but rather consistent kindness, yet firm if needed. I have learned that if a dog tries to bite, and you correct it in a manner they deem aggressive, it validates the bite, and makes them more on edge. Instead, ignore the actions, keep yourself safe, but don't respond to that behavior, just reset the dog as you need it, take a deep breath and continue. I always explain that the owner doesn't need to feel shame or embarrassment for how the dog acts, as this is a strange process and that I am a stranger doing things out of the norm, and invading the dogs personal space. This alone is breaking the dogs code of interactions. Become the anchor for the dogs emotions, and they will evolve. Being the anchor simply means to keep your inner self calm and open in a peaceful manner.

When ready to work with Penny, I got her owner to pick her up and place her on the table. I slipped on the neck strap, and she began to quiver. I had an earbud in one ear playing peaceful meditation music as a feed into my brain to be like water, and follow her lead. (While working with dogs I rarely speak to them, instead, in my mind I imagine loving words, and remind them they are safe. My focus is all energy based, soft eyes, soft mouth, sometimes licking lips and yawning, as this is the body language dogs use to calm their body).

I did my pre-brush with the coat king, clipped her nails, and she just stood there shaking, but no resistance. Then I took her to the bath, washed her up, brought her to the table wrapped in a towel, cleaned her ears, and all this time I envisioned love around her. I filled my heart with loving thoughts, so she could feel it emanating outwardly to her. I placed the hoodie around her ears, and began to slowly blow dry her back end. In the few moments of this, I felt the energy shift, and her body went heavy. The owner and I looked at her face and her eyes were closed, her head was down, and her body had softened. She was resting into the moment. She allowed me to dry her, clip her coat down, and she never budged. This moment was and has been powerful for our relationship. Since that day 4 years ago, Penny always loves to see me. She still runs off when it is time to get on the table, but she trusts in our process and allows me to groom her without any fuss. Once she is placed back on the floor after grooming, she always runs to show her owners, and then comes back and gives me affection. She feels safe with the experience, and that is the key to our relationship.

When talking with her owner in reflection to what was different, he said the other groomer was so busy, it was loud and there was lots of chaos in the shop. She was rushed and just put Penny on the table. But without allowing Penny to process her environment, this caused her to panic. She tried to get away, and used all her known tools to do so, which were barking, squirming and biting. It took just moments for an already emotionally taxed groomer to give up and send her home. This scenario is a common one, where the environment is not conducive to calm. And it is the groomer's responsibility to change it.

Shift the environment by removing the idea that this is an industrialized business, and create a spa-like energy. Staff and dogs will respond better, and the results will be an increase in better clients and an increase in income.

A dog can tell when a human/ another dog is upset, happy, sad or excited. This is energy, and a good approach for groomers is to treat dogs as energy meridians. They decide their own fate, how fast they will warm up and allow touches. Sounds crazy I know, but think about it. This is a living creature, whose trust is being put into your hands to groom, to care for, with so many sights, smells and physical sensations- they have every right to take their time to feel safe. Grooming is scary for dogs for many reasons. Being left behind by their owners, all the new smells, loud sounds, being in the care of someone they don't know, and to be cleaned, handled and groomed is a lot for anyone. Also, grooming is fairly invasive, causing dogs to be handled and touched in manners that don't typically happen in their home life, which invades their physical and emotional space. So having patience is important. Taking control of your emotions is valuable for you, the client and the owner.

Think of it as going to the doctors' office. You can go in very sick, receive care to become healthier, but while you sit there you are in an uncomfortable and unpleasant emotional space. Though the reason you seek a doctor is for a better outcome, the action may be unpleasant until the treatment is complete. It is the same with grooming, we remove sensitive ear hair, eye hair, hair under paw pads, and around their genitals. Dogs don't know why this is happening, and we can't tell them. What we can do is hold our own energy in a peaceful loving state, because dogs can feel emotions. Give them the gift of your calm state.

Self-assessment is the best tool to begin making positive changes. You are doing great for taking the steps.

When you meet a new client, look at the owners' energy, and think of loving thoughts while you do. So acknowledge their concerns with a kind heart, and allow them to be heard. The dog is taking cues from their owner while in your presence. The dog is watching to see if the situation is safe, and if you don't make the owner feel at peace, the dog will not feel at peace either. A lot of new clients are nervous when going to a shop for the first time. Their mind is full of horror stories they have read about dogs being injured or mistreated by groomers. So offer them the calm that you are safe, their preconceived ideas have nothing to do with you, they want to find a loving safe space to work with their dog. So offer them that.

Everytime you put a dog on your table, treat it as if it is the first time. Give them the ability to warm up to the process. Introduce the brush and take a moment to brush the dog prior to bathing. Let them find safety in you. Once you have made that connection, then you can proceed with other tasks. This integration on the table is important in preparing the dogs mind to what is happening.

A technique to use if the dogs' energy is very busy and you feel that you're struggling to stay calm, is to breathe in deeply while imagining calm energy filling your lungs and exhale while imagining the anxious, busy thoughts leaving your body. Do this two or three times and gather yourself.

We are the caretaker of ourselves and the animals that come to our table. It is our main job to keep them safe. You will see over time using intentional actions, that your spirit lifts, and the whole experience changes.

I remember years ago when I would work with aggressive dogs, my energy would be so depleted and I would cry at the end of the day to release it. I found that as I was working with them, I would be unconsciously taking on their emotions, trying to give them ease within their bodies. But the reality is that I was destroying myself, because I was meeting them at their level. Now when I work with dogs who are aggressive, I stay calm, and breathe deeply and send that big energy to something beyond myself. I don't take responsibility to hold it for the dog, but rather I maintain my calm, and allow the dog to have all its big emotions, and in my mind, I imagine it dissipating into the universe. This may sound strange but your brain doesn't know the difference between reality and so by you using imagery in your mind, you really can make big shifts in your reality. Perception is your reality. So you can teach yourself mind games to help move through stressful situations.

Yesterday I went to groom a dog I have been working with for a few years now. We will call the dog Bob. Bob has always had aggression on the table, and this past year he has been getting worse with being handled. He did have one bad experience at another shop when a puppy, but I have been his primary groomer the majority of his life. When I first met him, he was trying to bite. I explained to the owners that I needed to allow his emotions to come through, and I will work with him in the safest manner I can. I groom in the owners home, and know they are lovely people who care greatly about Bob. Bobs behaviour is not for me to psychoanalyze. But I know it isn't from mistreatment, but rather genetics as he is coming to an age where these things arise. The last year he has become unmanageable on the table, where we are at a point that he needs to be medicated to work on. I have been transparent with Bob's owners that he always needs muzzling, and sometimes his face is left half done, and his groom looks like a drunken uncle took clippers to him. They still pay, and continue to call me back, because I have told them the truth, and they trust me. My rates are premium, and when working with aggression, there is a topper added onto base rates. I have been paid on the two times I showed up, and he was too agitated to even get a muzzle on, so the appointment was canceled. And this is because of the way I cultivate clients in my life, and the communication and respect we have, that they pay and value my opinion. I have never shamed them for how Bob is, I work with them, offering tips and tools to help. I reschedule, and am always polite. Yesterday I went and groomed him. We had set up that he would be given sedation, and the owner bought a muzzle prior so he could have it on Bob before I arrived. It was agreed that the husband would help hold and support Bob while I groomed him. This shows me their dedication to the dogs needs. When arriving, I go over how we will work together. When he is apologetic about Bobs aggression, I hear him and reassure him that we can't undo Bobs being, but we can find a way to best support Bob. Together we get Bob groomed, face partially shaved around the muzzle, nails done and body shaved down. My job is to control the entire situation, guiding the owner to breathe and find calm, and regulate myself and also groom. We got it done, new price was paid, and the owners were happy. And it wasn't pretty, Bob was trying to bite the entire time, screaming, and jumping around. But it is a grey zone where the dog needs grooming as it is a hair breed, and I know I have the capacity to hold loving space while working in a high stress environment. We agreed next time he requires a larger dose of sedation, and that I would be back in three months. When you read this what judgments arise? These owners have had him groomed every 6-8 weeks for years and now we spread it out longer to 12 weeks as Bob has so much reaction to the grooming.Medically pain has been ruled out, although I have suspicions his front legs are bowed, that they could be tender. Sometimes genetics play a role in the behavior of a dog, also there can be generational trauma within that animal that causes them to react in such a way. Scientists have found that the body can hold traumatic responses up to 3 generations, so it is not unrealistic to say that a dog can also have what seems like irrational responses to situations.

There are many situations like this that I come across, where the owners are lovely, they are not neglectful, and really want the best for their animals. It is an honour to be trusted to work with them, because the other option is complete sedation, which over the long-term is more harmful to the body for animals.

I am not suggesting everyone work with dogs who are high risk, but what I am saying is, if we communicate and are transparent with clients, they will become great clients, and you will be able to work with all kinds of dogs and have better relationships with the owners.

The rebuilding of trust with clients is learning how to communicate and cultivate good relationships through the way you speak and emotionally show up. It takes time to retrain the brain to think like this, but it works and can be done.

CHAPTER 7
Not All Dogs Are The Same

"Dogs do speak, but only to those who know how to listen."– Orhan Pamuk

Every dog has its story, a way it has traveled through life, how it sees each person. It is our responsibility to adjust how we are to create safety, so they can settle and find peace in our energy. We bring the energy, and they respond to it.

Penny from the previous chapter seems like a one off story, but I have seen it time and time again over my entire grooming career. So many dogs are kicked out of shops, mistreated and mislabeled and it's almost always the energy of the room and the groomer. We can't choose how the dog will be, but we can choose how we will respond. When an owner brings a dog to you, you can choose to work with love, and integrity. And when you're unsure, come to this thought:

"Who do I need to be in this moment to make this better?"

A dog is biting. It is best not to respond with anger, but rather be in a safe space. Lower your gaze, soften your shoulders, relax your jaw, turn away from the dog, and just stay still. Or if that isn't possible as the dog is on the table, freeze what you are doing, turn away from the head of the dog, and face its back end. Hold the rear of the dog so it won't swing off the table, and just focus on your breath.

Four count box breathing. Breathe into the count of four, hold for the count of four, exhale to the count of four, hold for the count of four. Repeat this 4 times, or longer if needed. When you regulate yourself, this co-regulates those around you- animals included.

The phrase 'Who do I need to be at this moment ?' is the answer to everything. This is what you would need at the moment, so offer that to the dog. There is no room for ego on the grooming table. We have learned throughout the book how to look inward and clear out our own clutter, so we can be safe spaces for the dogs we work with.

Begin trusting in yourself, and responding to the dogs and owners with what you would have needed in the same position. Ask yourself, what does this dog need, what tools can I use to make the pet feel safe and comfortable during the grooming process? If a dog is anxious and nervous, giving them a break, or taking an alternative approach can make the difference. Instead of pushing through with force and aggression, take a minute to calm yourself, and then approach the dog with softer energy. Speak in a calm and soothing tone, move slowly and give the dog room to adjust and respond. Sometimes just acknowledging the dog's emotions and allowing them to express it can be enough to calm them down. Remember, we don't have to solve every problem right away, but showing empathy and understanding can go a long way in building trust with the dog. In addition, it's important to remember that not all dogs are the same. Some may have had traumatic experiences in the past that make them more anxious or fearful during grooming. It's crucial to approach each dog with an open mind and be prepared to adjust your techniques and methods accordingly. And sometimes, it may not even be the dog that needs to change, it could be us as the groomer. We may need to change our own mindset or approach to better accommodate the needs of the dog. A great way to learn more about dog behavior and communication is to study the different body language and signals that dogs use. There are many resources available online or through books that can help you understand what the dogs are showing you. This knowledge will not only help you build a great rapport with current clients but also future ones.

Senior dogs tend to be dismissed quite frequently from salons because of their age and the fear that they are old and will get injured on the table. It's not because of the age issue, but more lack of trust in one's self, and also the communication with the owners. As dogs age, we need to remember to adjust- which means our rate may increase to cover the longer time needed, the quality of the cut may change as the most important thing is less stress. So quicker cut and less fuss as your energy and time is spent more in supporting a senior client vs haircut. Clients are ok with this approach, and many prefer to do what is best for the dog vs a fancy haircut.

Factors to look at are time , the dog's ability , and cost.

Say that you have groomed a dog since puppy- puppy rates should be higher as you're training and they are often squirming around. Once the dog has settled into the process, drop the rate or keep it the same. Once a dog is requiring more time from soreness, dementia, and anxiety from aging, then adjust the price for that shift and also decrease the owner's expectations on the groom that the dog receives. Most owners, if they knew the stress of a senior dog on a table for 1-1.5hr being groomed, would be ok with it if you shortened the time to 45 minutes and took out fluff drying or the detailed work you would do prior.

When we shift the little things, it can bring peace to the animals and ourselves as we work.

Dogs want peace, they lean into ease, so if we want a smooth relationship with them, we need to be fluid with how we work. Our persistence to keep pushing in a direction that isn't working gives back resistance. When we lean into ease, things open up.

I have found in my career that affirmations help shift the energy while working. So if a dog is anxious, I will softly repeat "you are safe, you are loved". And this simple act shifts my mind and the dogs' energy.

These tools, although seemingly not linked to grooming, will help you in career and also life. Becoming an anchor for energetic beings is how one controls the mood of a room. When you have gained control of your own energy, other beings will gravitate to meet you there. That is the power you possess within.

Creating a safe and nurturing environment for dogs during grooming is more than just a technical skill; it involves a deep understanding of their emotional states and the ability to adapt to their unique personalities. For example, a once-exuberant pup might transform into a hesitant senior, struck by the weight of years spent in an unpredictable world. In such cases, the groomer must act as both caregiver and confidant, reading the dog's body language as if it were a complex script. Recognizing subtle signs of discomfort—like a lowered tail or tense posture—allowing for adjustments in approach, from the tools we choose to the tempo of our movements.

As we prepare for a grooming session, it's important to remember that each interaction is a shared experience. Establishing a dialogue with the dog, even if it feels one-sided, lays the groundwork for mutual understanding. Use your hands not just to groom, but to be gentle and use reassuring strokes that convey warmth and safety. When we express patience and kindness, we create a space where trust can flourish.

Moreover, when managing a diverse clientele, using open and honest communication with dog owners is essential. Educate them about their dog's needs, addressing any concerns they might have. Oftentimes, simply conveying how important it is to prioritize comfort over aesthetics can shift owners' perspectives, allowing them to embrace a more compassionate approach. As groomers, we become not just service providers but advocates for the well-being of our canine companions, nurturing a sense of community built on trust, empathy, and love. The journey toward ensuring every dog feels valued and understood is a shared goal, and it starts with each thoughtful interaction we make.

CHAPTER 8

How To Set You Value

"Be brutally honest about the short-term and be optimistic and confident about the long term" Reed Hastings

Pricing isn't just about covering costs; it's a powerful declaration of your worth, a reflection of your dedication, and a strategic tool to build a thriving business. It's the point where your hard-earned expertise, continuous education, and significant investments translate into tangible rewards. But it's not just about dollars and cents; it's about the emotional exchange, the peace of mind you provide to pet owners, and the well-being of the dogs entrusted to your care.

Choosing the right rates to draw in the clients is important, but understanding the psychology behind those prices is equally crucial. As you navigate the complexities of setting your pricing structure, consider not only the tangible services you offer, but also the emotional advantages your clients both human and canine, will experience. This is not merely about dollars and cents. This encompasses the well-being of the pets in your care, and the peace of mind of their owners.

The Psychology of Pricing:

Begin by conducting market research to grasp what others in your area are charging for similar services. This provides a foundation to build your pricing on, but don't hesitate to adjust according to your unique qualifications and the specialized services you provide. A higher price can communicate quality, but ensure it aligns with the value you deliver. Are you incorporating advanced training techniques? Unique grooming styles? Perhaps you offer personalized consultations for anxious or aggressive dogs that truly sets you apart. Emphasizing these elements in your marketing can attract owners seeking more than just standard care. They will see that you are an expert committed to elevating their dog's quality of life.

Value-Based Pricing and Storytelling:

Lastly, embrace the art of storytelling in your pricing justification. Use testimonials from satisfied clients who have witnessed significant transformations in their dogs through your services. Incorporating real stories not only humanizes your business, but also demonstrates the value, painting a vivid picture that makes your pricing feel justified and fair. As you refine your rates, remember that it is just as much an invitation into a new relationship as it is a transaction—one that signifies your commitment to nurturing the well-being of every dog that crosses your threshold.

Your Personal Worth and Happiness:

Remember, your happiness matters. If you dread a particular job, charge a premium that makes it worthwhile. If the client agrees, excellent. If not, you've protected your energy and maintained your integrity. Don't compromise your worth for the sake of filling your schedule.

In-Home vs. Shop Pricing: Positioning Your Brand:

A shop has a different pricing system than grooming pets at home. Usually, in-home grooming costs more because it's a one-on-one service, and you can only care for a few dogs in a day. This is a premium service, and you need to believe in its value. Shop prices can be higher if you present yourself as high value. Clients judge services based on what you show them. If you want to be seen as a luxury brand, like a Maserati rather than a basic car like a Prius, then shape your business accordingly.

My Personal Pricing Philosophy:

Education and skill is one part, but it's also your ability to work with clients and owners. People support those they feel a connection with, so the more you heal yourself, the better you show up as an authentic person, and the more you are trusted.

I split dogs into many categories- I have my base rate which I believe I am worth minimally. So to groom any dog, the minimum is $150. If it takes me 30 minutes or one hour, it is that base rate. That covers drive time, set up and interaction with clients. Then, if the dog is larger, squirmy, or aggressive, I tack on other rates for time. These rates are not necessarily forever, but at least until the dog stops having the responses which make my job harder.

Temperament-Based Pricing: You should also charge for the dog's temperament, especially if the dog is aggressive. Let clients know in advance that there is a handling fee for these dogs. Most people just want to make sure you're safe, so it's important to have honest conversations with them. Be clear about how you will work with their dog and explain that you'll do your best to keep the dog calm while still giving a good haircut, but there are limits to what can be done in one grooming session.

- **Transparent Communication:** Be upfront with clients about these fees. Explain the rationale and emphasize your commitment to their dog's well-being.

Aggressive dogs have a $40-100 rate on top of groom rate. This is because there is a high risk of injury. With the increase, I have time to give the dog the patience and care it requires. I never recommend someone who doesn't have training in aggression to work with dogs who have high bite risk. Instead, always refer to a groomer trained in it. If you do have an interest to learn, give time to each appointment and be prepared to practice inner calm a lot. This can be tricky if you're newly starting out.

- **Referral Network:** Recognize your limits. If you lack experience with aggressive dogs, refer them to a trained professional.

- **Incremental Growth:** Plan for gradual price increases ($5-$10 annually) to reflect your growing expertise and the rising cost of living.

Think of where you want to be in 5 years. What rate would make you happy? Now charge back to now. At $5-10 price increase per year, drop down to now. $150 per dog, start at $100 per dog. Set clauses for aggressive dogs, matted coats, or skin issues, as those add extra time so need an extra fee.

Keep it simple, and straight forward. Include all the services in the base fee, bath, blow dry, nails clipped, ears cleaned. Then if you need a haircut, or a de-shed, these are two separate things.

Building Trust and Client Loyalty:

The more you improve yourself, the more you can charge for your services. While location is somewhat important, people will travel if they recognize your value. Getting reviews from clients is crucial. Encourage your clients to leave reviews on your Google page. Having a Google page is essential because it helps clients find you, see examples of your work, and read reviews. When potential clients understand what you offer for the price, they are more likely to trust you and spend their money.

Establishing a genuine connection with your clients is not just a matter of pleasant conversation; it's a critical skill that influences their perception of value in your services. For example, during an initial consultation, take a moment to engage with the owner about their dog's unique personality. Ask about their preferences, routines, and any past grooming experiences—good or bad. This dialogue not only opens the door for mutual understanding but also sets the stage for trust. When clients feel seen and heard, they are more likely to accept your suggested rates, because they will realize the care and expertise underpinning each grooming session.

Ongoing Dialogue and Adaptation:

Pricing is not static. Reassess your rates every nine months, reflecting on your growth and ensuring alignment with your values. Ask yourself: Am I charging what I'm worth? Am I providing premium care?

Actionable Strategies:

- Create tiered pricing based on dog temperament and service complexity.
- Develop a script for explaining handling fees for aggressive dogs.

- Design a client feedback system to gather testimonials and reviews.
- Craft a pricing guide that highlights your unique value proposition.
- Schedule regular reviews of your pricing strategy to ensure it reflects your growth and market conditions.

By embracing these strategies, you'll not only set profitable prices but also cultivate lasting client relationships built on trust, transparency, and a shared commitment to canine well-being."

Additionally, consider crafting a pricing structure that reflects not only the services provided but also the emotional energy and expertise you bring to the table. For instance, instead of simply listing rates, you might describe the thoughtful approach you take with aggressive or anxious dogs. Illustrate how your practices, grounded in patience and empathy, ensure a safer and calmer experience for both the pet and the groomer. By sharing anecdotes or testimonials from clients who have witnessed these transformations, you create a compelling narrative that enhances the perceived value of your work.

Remember, pricing is an ongoing dialogue, not a static figure. Set aside regular intervals—perhaps every nine months—to reassess your rates and reflect on your growth. Ask yourself: Do I feel aligned with my current prices? Am I confident that I'm providing premium care? By being adaptable and transparent about your pricing evolution, you will continue to shift the paradigm, not only for your business but for the grooming industry as a whole. This candid approach fosters a community of loyal clients who not only appreciate your artistry but also advocate for your services.

Trust in the process and trust in yourself.

CHAPTER 9
You Did It

Fantastic! You finished the book, made changes and are now actively participating in creating the life you want.

As we did at the beginning of the book, take your journal and write out a current perception of how you are and how you relate to your clients and work.

We went over what it can be like in a shop in chapter one. Not all are like this, but it instills a feeling within the body that most groomers have experienced at one point in their career, if not on the regular. Things weren't working for you, you took note, and took the step to make changes. Let's answer the following questions and see where you are at.

This phase is to paint a current picture for yourself of where your mind is now. To give you an idea of where you were and where you have expanded. So grab a journal and a pen, and write on the top of the page in bold letters **HAVE GRACE FOR MYSELF**. And remember that as you begin to answer these questions.

Let's begin at this moment. Remove judgment, and see your reality for what it is.

I ask you to soften your eyes and honestly write out a snippet of you.

How do you see yourself?

How do you think others see you? (friends, clients, family)

How do you dress for work? What feelings arise when choosing clothes for work? Is the outfit expressing who you are, and what you want to portray to the world?

Do you dress for the person you want to be, or the person of the now? Do you dress in a manner you assume groomers should dress?

Are you happy, content, and fulfilled? Or sad, dreading the day, and having low energy?

Do you treat customers with joy, or as a hassle? Are you energized to see them, or glum?

If you were a possible client and walked into your shop as it is at this moment- would you want to have your pet there? If so, write out what is working, and if not, write out what isn't working for you.

Are you nourishing your mind and body with healthy choices? Or are you consuming nutritionally void foods, and filling your mind with stagnant things like news, gossip, and distracting shows?

What are the daily thoughts in your mind?

Do you feel happy after completing a groom? Do you feel pride in your work?

Are you showing up the best you can?

Are there blind spots contributing to your lack of being where you want to be?

What kind of human interactions do you have in your life? In your home, work and in social settings.

What are your current earnings? Are you satisfied with that?

If you have employees or work with others, what is your standard way of being with them? What are the common conversations? What is the mood in the shop when everyone is together?

What type of clients do you attract?

How is the current state of your shop (state of equipment , smell of the shop, vibe of the shop? Is it organized, or in disarray?

What is the current state of your car (is maintenance and upkeep done regularly, are engine lights on, what is the smell of the car, organized, or in disarray)?

What is the current state of your home (state of items you have, smell of the home, does it feel welcoming, organized, or in disarray)?

How is the current state of your life now? Write out the first word that comes to mind.

If you were a possible client and walked into your shop as it was- would you want to have your pet there? If so, write out what is working, and if not, write out what isn't working for you?

Where do you want to see yourself in 6 months, 12 months and 5 years from now (if there was a magic wand, where would you be)?

What was most apparent in your transitions between timelines?

What are the skills you have now?

Which skills would you like to obtain in the future, in 6 months, 12 months and 5 years?

What are your weaknesses? What do you feel you can improve on? Can that be taken over by another member of the team, or hired out for someone else to do? If not, then can you increase your skills, so they become strengths. You get the chance to change your reality by evolving skills or mindset.

Which clients bring you the most joy? I love to journal out my dream clients, and then I look at how I treat them, and I begin treating the others the same way, and very quickly the clients who weren't my dream ones, shift and become amazing. If we treat each client as our favourite, and only speak goodness of them, then they become that. Keep that in mind.

What dogs are you best at grooming, and why? How can you get more of those clients, so you can be doing more of what you are best at?

What would I like to earn per day/week/month? How can you get to that rate? Adjust prices, upgrade skills, re-brand?

What I want to be working: Are you working a schedule that feels good for you? If not, I ask you to challenge yourself and make a change

Who do you think people see you as? How others see us does matter when running a business. We often think our unconscious mind is running maladaptive behaviours which we call "personality" and give blame to that; but the reality is, we are more than that. So when we unload the layers and show up as our whole selves, then people will appreciate us for who we truly are. So who do you think they see?

Where are you now in life? Are you set up in a manner you're proud of, or is there more that you would like?

What am I unthankful for; how can I change it?

Write it in a manner of releasing.

I release all that does not serve me for my highest good.

I release my clients who bring unkind words to the shop

I release the dogs who don't align with me

I release anger that I hold inside

I release the feeling of self sabotage

I release the fear of not paying my bills

I release the overwhelming request of the clients

I release frustration I feel when friends ask me for discounts and I can't say no

Write a list of gratitude for what you have. Putting to paper what we have gives us the chance to see with our eyes the blessings before us. Some may have larger lists than others, but having gratitude for what WE have is key.   You can desire more, but need to be grateful for what you have, or else nothing will satisfy. In this gratitude list also write out what you wish to achieve, but write it in the present tense.

I am thankful for the high salary of $xxx,xxx that I earn.

I am thankful for my clients' appreciation of what an amazing service I offer.

I am thankful for the ease each day brings, and how it flows with joy.

I am thankful for my strong body that helps complete my tasks.

I am thankful for my overflowing support from my clients.

I am thankful etc...

After all of this, flip back to the first of your journal, and see the changes. This is you doing it all!! You owe yourself a hug, and thank yourself for becoming the version of yourself that you desire to be. And for that I acknowledge you and your efforts.

What did you see as the biggest shift through the book? Reflect back to your journal and goals on a regular bases. Keep going on the inner growth and watch your world open up.

As you sit down to embrace the possibilities ahead, the weight of your journey lifts, leaving space for clarity and creativity. Journaling has become your sanctuary—a place to sculpt not only your thoughts but also your future ambitions. In the flickering light of your workspace, you start to map out the vibrant visions you hold for your grooming career and, more importantly, for the connections you cultivate with each dog and their owner. With each stroke of your pen, you visualize the thriving business you desire. Six months from now, you can see yourself confidently balancing your schedule, working with diverse clients who resonate with your values. A year ahead, you'll have expanded your skill set, perhaps mastering innovative grooming techniques that will set your service apart. Five years down the line, financial stability and client loyalty will be your reality, with the promise of growth ahead.

Yet, it's not just the goals that matter; it's the layers of self-awareness you're peeling back. You reflect on your weaknesses, recognizing them not as burdens but as stepping stones for mastery. You've learned it's okay to ask for help—whether it's outsourcing tasks or dedicating time for personal skill enhancement. As you ponder the joy-giving clients, you note their unique qualities. They inspire you to treat every client with that same fervor, cultivating an atmosphere of positivity that transforms even the most challenging of circumstances. This conscious shift mirrors the way you engage with the dogs in your care; each interaction is an opportunity to bridge trust and understanding, making these precious moments fulfilling.

With gratitude flooding your heart, you write your list, affirming not just what you have, but what you are becoming. The ink flows easily, filled with the appreciation of your growth. You acknowledge every small victory—the day when a timid pup found solace in your hands, or when a grateful owner showered you with praise. "I am thankful for the joy of helping each dog reveal their best selves," you write, allowing the ink to etch your commitment to this journey deeper. As you lean back, pausing to absorb the energy of your words, you smile; the path may twist, but your course remains clear. You've done it. You're evolving, and the best is yet to come.

www.ingramcontent.com/pod-product-compliance
Lightning Source LLC
Chambersburg PA
CBHW020341010526
44119CB00048B/558